MASTERING THE ART OF LETTING GO OF WORRY AND OVERTHINKING

A ROADMAP TO INNER PEACE AND MENTAL CLARITY

DAVID M. TURNER

This Book Belong To

....

CONTENTS

THE PREVALENCE OF WORRY AND OVERTHINKING

I t seems sense that anxiety and overthinking have become unwanted companions on our life's journey in a world where things are moving faster than ever, information is all around us and our duties appear to be piling up every day. These heavy mental habits have a tendency of becoming a part of who we are from the moment we wake up till we lay our heads down. We are imprisoned by the never-ending "what ifs" and repeat of past choices, which keeps us from fully enjoying life's happiness and tranquility.

The Effect on Emotional and Mental Health

Overanalyzing and worrying are not just peculiarities of the human mind. They are enemies who cause great harm to our lives by undermining our mental and emotional health. These thought patterns cause ongoing upheaval that permeates not just our bodies but also our thoughts, providing a fertile foundation for tension, worry and even physical health issues. Our hyperactive thoughts have a detrimental effect on our relationships, both personal and professional, frequently resulting in misunderstandings and alienation.

Specifically, overthinking impairs our ability to make decisions. It impairs our ability to solve problems, distorts our judgment and paralyzes our activities. Our worries grow heavier and pull us farther from the composed, collected people we want to be the longer we concentrate on them and allow them to fester.

The Prospect of Mental Clarity and Inner Peace

But the goal of this book is to show the way toward a happier, more peaceful future, not to wallow in the misery that worry and overanalyzing can bring. The promise of mental clarity and inner serenity is a ray of hope, proof of the capacity of the human spirit to rise above hardship and realize its full potential.

As a psychologist and personal development specialist, I have seen innumerable people emerge from the mud of excessive concern and overanalysis to find a life of calm and clarity. Not only is this path feasible, but it is also attainable for each and every one of us. The first steps in changing oneself are realizing where these sneaky habits come from and developing a strong enough mentality to resist their hold.

This book serves as your road map for escaping the confines of anxiety and overanalyzing. It will walk you through the complexities of your mind and provide useful, doable techniques for developing mental clarity and inner serenity. We shall go through the choppy waters of the mind together, discovering how to calm its restlessness and realize how profoundly peaceful we really are.

Are you prepared to start this life-changing adventure? Come learn the skill of letting go, open the door to mental clarity and inner calm and experience a life of freedom and fulfillment that beyond your wildest expectations.

CHAPTER 1

UNDERSTANDING WORRY AND OVERTHINKING

What Worry and Overthinking Really Mean

A thorough awareness of these mental foes is essential to learning the discipline of letting go of stress and overthinking. What exactly are they? We use these terms carelessly a lot of the time, treating them like little annoyances that can be ignored. But they are lot more subtle and pernicious than they seem at first.

Essentially, worry is the result of an innate protection mechanism in our brains. It is a survival strategy that many generations of evolution have ingrained in our minds. Our predecessors used worry to weigh the risks, act quickly and ultimately assure their survival when faced with life-threatening circumstances. Once useful in the wild, this instinctive reaction has now become complex and multifaceted. Even if worry used to be well-intentioned, it has now grown excessive and illogical, resulting in tension and anxiety that frequently have no use.

Conversely, overthinking is the compulsive need to go over, rethink and examine every choice and situation. It resembles an obsessive investigator who never shuts up. It can be helpful in moderation, guiding our decision-making. But when overthinking gets out of hand, it may be crippling and keep us from moving forward at all.

Overanalyzing and Anxiety: The Psychology Behind It

We need to study the psychology of anxiety and overanalyzing in order to become proficient in the art of letting go. These behaviors frequently have their origins in deeply rooted anxieties, traumatic experiences from the past, or social pressures. Disarming these behaviors' hold over us begins with an understanding of their psychological foundations.

Anxiety, which is closely related to excessive worry, is caused by an inflated perception of threats, an inability to control the future, or a dread of the unknown. Our thoughts, trying to keep us safe, endlessly generate "what if" scenarios that paralyze us with a never-ending sense of dread. As the complexities of the human psyche are solved, worry is revealed to be an improper natural reaction—a signal from our inner selves demanding our attention.

Overanalyzing also has strong psychological foundations. It usually has its roots in the fear of making errors or being judged by others. This never-ending examination is motivated by an insatiable desire for clarity and a desire to steer clear of uncertainty. We are better able to break free from the grip that overthinking has on our life the more we comprehend the reasons and triggers that lead to it.

Recognizing Patterns and Triggers

Being able to recognize the patterns and triggers that lead to concern and overthinking is essential to the process of learning how to let go. These triggers are as unique as the people who encounter them and there are many ways in which patterns can appear. By identifying them, we may break the pattern and take back control of our thoughts.

External triggers include things like environmental pressures and challenging life situations. They may also come from within, rooted in our ideas, convictions and prior encounters. Gaining the upper hand in a fight against an unseen foe is similar to learning to identify these triggers.

The recurrent thought patterns that keep us anxious and overthinking are called patterns. Rumination, perfectionism and catastrophic thinking are a few examples of these. We may start the process of breaking these tendencies and creating new, better mental habits by recognizing them.

We will delve deeper into these aspects of anxiety and overthinking in the upcoming chapters, providing you with the information and resources you need to defeat these enemies once and for all. By gaining understanding, we set the stage for the change that is just around the corner and are led in the direction of the prospect of inner serenity and mental clarity.

CHAPTER 2

THE TOLL ON HEALTH AND HAPPINESS

Physical and Emotional Consequences

The harsh truth of the negative effects worry and overthinking have on our happiness and health must be faced if one is to genuinely learn how to let go of these bad habits. The effect is not limited to the intellect; it ripples across all facets of our lives, touching every area of our welfare.

First and foremost, extended concern and overthinking have serious negative effects on one's health. Our bodies suffer greatly from the constant stress reaction, which releases a series of hormones that lead to a wide range of illnesses. Unchecked anxiety can have far-reaching and perhaps fatal consequences, ranging from immune system damage to cardiovascular problems.

What's as important are the emotional fallout. Our emotional supplies are eroded by worry and overanalyzing, leaving us emotionally weak and empty. Our self-esteem and general emotional resilience are undermined when we become caught up in a never-ending loop of self-doubt and critical self-talk. Constant anxiety can cause impatience, withdrawal and misunderstandings with loved ones, which damages relationships. The emotional fallout from these events is a tremendous load.

Case Studies and Empirical Illustrations

As a specialist in the area, I have had the honor of assisting people from a variety of backgrounds who are battling anxiety and overthinking in their own special ways. During my professional experience, I have personally observed the palpable and frequently disastrous consequences of these behaviors. Permit me to tell you the tales of others who have faced and overcome these challenges.

Meet Sarah, a young professional whose anxiety of making errors and her incessant need for confirmation have held back her promising career. Her tendency to overthink things prevented her from taking initiative, which resulted in lost chances and stagnant personal development.

Or take John, a father who found it difficult to enjoy life on a daily basis since he was constantly concerned about his children's future. He was unable to let go of these worries, which kept him from being totally present and interacting with his family.

These are just a few instances of the innumerable lives that are trapped in the mazes of anxiety and overanalyzing. They provide as tangible evidence of the urgent need for change.

The Immediate Need for Adjustment

Nobody should have to suffer the negative effects of worry and overthinking on their health and happiness. It is impossible to exaggerate the need for change. If we keep going in the same direction, we will let priceless moments pass us by, maintain a cycle of self-inflicted agony and lower the standard of our lives.

The prospect of mental clarity and inner calm is not some far-off dream; rather, it is a very real potential that is within reach. It is a promise of a life freed from needless worry and one filled with the small joys of everyday living. Change is not only something we want; it is a basic need for living a life that is meaningful.

We will discuss how to break free from these bonds and put health and happiness back where they belong in your life in the pages that follow. Although the road requires bravery and dedication, the benefits are enormous. Accompany me on this journey and together we will discover the way to a happier, more fulfilling life.

CHAPTER 3

THE ROADMAP TO INNER PEACE

Mindfulness and Present-Centered Awareness

The practice of mindfulness and present-centered awareness is essential to learning how to let go of stress and overthinking. In your quest for inner peace, these practices will be your allies, keeping you grounded in the present now rather than becoming bogged down in the rabbit holes of the past and future.

Developing a keen awareness of and acceptance of the current moment without passing judgment is the essence of mindfulness. It invites you to meet your ideas, feelings and experiences head-on as they come up. By practicing mindfulness, you can lessen the influence that your anxieties and ideas have over your mind by learning to observe them objectively. This exercise promotes mental clarity and a deeper appreciation for the small pleasures in life.

Including mindfulness in your everyday activities can have a profoundly positive impact. It helps you to escape the never-ending loop of overanalyzing by gently bringing your attention back to the here and now. I will give you helpful exercises and advice on incorporating mindfulness into your life as a subject matter expert in order to empower you to take control of your thoughts and direct them toward inner serenity.

Letting Go and Acceptance

Inner serenity is supported by the twin pillars of acceptance and letting go. These techniques help you recognize your fears and concerns and give you the confidence to let go of them when they become too much for you. They are about learning to live with the thoughts that trouble you and finding the courage to let them go into the stream of life.

A deep grasp of what you can and cannot control is what is meant by acceptance, not resignation. You can free yourself from the pointless effort to alter the unchangeable by embracing the truths of life. This procedure helps you find peace of mind and eases your mental burden.

On the other side, letting go takes bravery and will. It entails letting go of your attachment to your anxieties and giving them time to pass. This surrender is a statement of power rather than weakness. I'll walk you through each step of the exercise and give you the skills you need to let go of your fears and give your mind a breather.

Resources for Fostering Inner Peace

You will have a toolkit full of techniques for developing inner calm as you set out on your path to inner peace. These resources light your way through even the darkest mental storms, much like beacons. They will enable you to take command of your thoughts and feelings once more.

You'll come to rely on breathing exercises, relaxation methods and meditation activities. These tools have been refined and polished over decades, providing countless people with comfort and peace of mind. I will not only expose you to these tactics as a specialist in this area, but I will also provide you helpful advice on how to incorporate them into your everyday routine.

The path to inner serenity is a never-ending journey rather than a final destination. It requires commitment, repetition and an openness to change. But the reward is well worth the effort: a life of peace, clarity and a revitalized sense of direction. Come along with me as we explore these life-changing techniques in the upcoming chapters, uncovering the power of acceptance, mindfulness and the methods for developing inner peace. We will go confidently and purposefully together down the path that leads to inner serenity that awaits you.

CHAPTER 4

STRATEGIES TO CONQUER OVERTHINKING

Practical Techniques for Quieting the Mind

Developing a toolset of useful strategies to stop the mind's constant chatter is necessary to overcome overthinking. To begin this road of transformation, you must first learn to recover control over your thoughts and quiet the chatter that keeps you mired in uncertainty and fear.

Deep breathing exercises, grounding techniques and mindfulness practices are useful methods for calming the mind. When used consistently, these resources can assist you in regaining focus and letting go of your tendency to overthink. I'll walk you through each exercise, offering advice and guidance along the way to help you gain the mental fortitude needed to control your thoughts.

Being consistent is crucial. As a specialist in this area, I've witnessed innumerable people change their lives by adopting these practices into their everyday schedules. By doing this, you can lay the groundwork for mental peace, which will enable you to confront overthinking head-on.

Dismantling Adverse Thought Patterns

Negative thought habits that have been imprinted profoundly over time are often the cause of overthinking. These thought patterns increase anxiety, feed self-doubt and make it hard to trust your judgment. Identifying these tendencies and taking them on head-on is the second method for overcoming overthinking.

We will work together to discover how to recognize these harmful thought patterns, which include self-criticism, black-and-white thinking and catastrophizing. You'll discover how to analyze and question these thought patterns in order to swap them out for more sensible and beneficial ones. Through this method, you will be able to take back control of your thoughts and lessen the influence that overthinking has on your life.

One of the most important things you can do to go toward inner peace is to learn how to confront negative thinking habits. You will notice a significant change in how you view and interact with the world as you face and conquer these habits.

Developing Love for Oneself

A key to overcoming overthinking is to practice self-compassion. Many people who struggle with overthinking are also their own worst critics, punishing themselves for perceived shortcomings and holding themselves to impossible standards. The overthinking loop is fueled by this self-critical perspective.

Treating yourself with the same consideration and understanding that you would extend to a good friend is the foundation of cultivating self-compassion. It entails realizing that everyone makes mistakes and experiences periods of uncertainty and that perfection is an illusion. You can build a defense against overthinking's self-destructive tendencies by practicing self-compassion.

I'll lead you through activities and introspection to support the growth of self-compassion. You'll discover how to quiet your inner critic and start talking to yourself in a kinder, more loving way. This change will improve your emotional health and perspective on life in addition to relieving you of the need to overthink everything.

Your door to regaining mental freedom and enduring inner calm is through learning overthinking tactics. You can liberate yourself from the shackles of overthinking and enjoy a life of clarity and tranquility by learning useful methods for stilling the mind, confronting unfavorable thought patterns and developing self-compassion. Come along with me as we examine these game-changing tactics and set off on a path to a happier, more peaceful future.

MASTERING THE ART OF WORRY MANAGEMENT

Stress Reduction and Relaxation Techniques

Learning to reduce tension and relax is the first step towards developing worry management skills, which are essential to learning the art of letting go. Our lives are overflowing with obligations, deadlines and demands, which can provide an ideal environment for worry to proliferate. We have to learn how to calm the stress storm before we can calm the worry storm.

Your best defence against the constant stresses of contemporary life is to practice relaxation and stress reduction. By becoming proficient in these methods, you'll be able to stop anxiety from taking hold in addition to reducing the emotional and physical effects of stress. I will walk you through the process of creating relaxation techniques, such as progressive muscle relaxation, deep breathing exercises and mindfulness-based stress reduction, as I am an expert in this field.

When you apply these strategies to your everyday life, you'll be able to rebuild resilience and equilibrium. You'll become more adept at navigating life's storms and managing your worry will become a crucial aspect of your quest for inner peace.

Establishing a Stress-Free Space

An important but sometimes overlooked part of managing anxiety is setting up a worry-free environment. Our environment greatly affects how we feel, therefore in order to become adept at letting go, we need to create a space that encourages us on our path to inner serenity.

We'll look at methods for setting limits, organizing your work and clearing out your physical area. You may create a calm and serene space by simplifying your surroundings and reducing outside factors that may cause you to overthink and worry.

It is possible to create an environment free from worry outside of the physical world. It includes creating a network of friends and family who are there to support you, maintaining good relationships and communicating effectively.

These components are essential to your ability to control anxiety and preserve mental clarity.

The Significance of Adaptability and Resilience

Resilience and adaptability are essential components of inner strength while learning concern management. Difficulties are a given in life since life is erratic. While adaptation helps you thrive in the face of change, resilience helps you recover from setbacks.

I'll teach you techniques for strengthening your emotional fortitude and improving your problem-solving abilities, as well as methods for developing resilience and flexibility. You'll discover how to see failures as chances for personal development rather than as causes for concern.

Resilience and adaptation have an impact on society as a whole, including your relationships and career. Their significance goes beyond the individual. You can build a life that is more flexible, more capable of navigating the unknowns of the future and less prone to worry by developing these traits.

We will go into great detail on the nuances of worry management in this section, giving you the skills and information you need to quiet the clamor of worry and open the door to inner serenity. You will make significant progress toward a life characterized by mental clarity and emotional resilience by embracing stress reduction and relaxation practices, establishing a worry-free environment and strengthening your resilience and adaptability. Come along with me on this enlightening journey as we collectively learn the art of concern management.

CHAPTER 6

CULTIVATING MENTAL CLARITY

Concentration and Focus's Power

Developing mental clarity is the lighthouse that points the way to a purposeful and peaceful existence. Developing the ability to focus and concentrate is crucial in today's fast-paced environment, when there are many distractions and the mind frequently feels like a stormy sea.

Our ability to simplify our thoughts and focus our mental energy on the here and now is facilitated by focus and concentration. When developed, these abilities act as a counterbalance to the mayhem that results from overanalyzing, enabling us to escape the bonds of persistent ruminating.

I will share my knowledge as a specialist in this area to help you improve your concentration and focus. You'll discover useful methods and activities that help you take back control of your daydreaming thoughts. You will gain the skills necessary to become an expert at concentration through mindfulness exercises and focused instruction, enabling you to create a sanctuary of mental clarity in your everyday life.

Techniques for Making Decisions

The worst effect overthinking has on our ability to make decisions is one of the biggest problems it presents. The never-ending loop of uncertainty and self-analysis impairs our ability to make decisions with assurance and clarity. Developing good decision-making techniques is inextricably connected to cultivating mental clarity.

We shall examine the fundamentals of well-informed decision-making in this part. You'll discover how to evaluate choices, establish priorities and carefully consider the advantages and disadvantages of each alternative. Improved techniques for making decisions will help you make decisions faster and with less emotional upheaval from doubt and ambiguity.

By becoming proficient in these techniques, you will create the groundwork for a life free from the burden of excessive analysis and characterized by clarity and decisiveness.

Improved Capabilities for Solving Problems

The ability to solve problems effectively is the sign of mental clarity. It is a skill that gives us the ability to confidently and poised negotiate the complexities of life and meet obstacles head-on. Our capacity to solve problems effectively is frequently hampered by overthinking, as it can snare us in a maze of needless anxiety and self-doubt.

I will provide you a thorough toolkit to improve your problem-solving skills because I am an authority in the industry. We will explore methods for dissecting intricate problems, evaluating viable fixes and formulating a methodical strategy for problem-solving. These abilities will help you develop a strong sense of empowerment and self-assurance in addition to making you a more skilled problem solver.

Developing mental clarity involves deliberate effort to improve your ability to focus, make decisions more quickly and solve problems more effectively. It is not a passive process. Gaining mastery over these aspects of mental clarity will open the door to a purposeful and decisive life. Come along with me as we examine the transformational potential of concentration, judgment and problem-solving techniques and together let's go on a path toward a life characterized by resilience and mental clarity.

CHAPTER 7

OVERCOMING OBSTACLES AND RELAPSES

Dealing with Relapses and Setbacks

Learning to let go of stress and overthinking is a process that is not always straightforward. That's a continuous process and setbacks and relapses are possible. The secret to real mastery, though, is to understand how to handle these situations rather than trying to avoid them.

The ability to handle failures and relapses is crucial if you want to achieve long-lasting inner calm. You'll develop the ability to spot when you're reverting to old routines and use practical techniques to get back on track. I will provide you the skills to recognize the early warning indicators of a relapse and reroute your path back toward clarity and tranquility as a subject matter expert in this area.

Being able to handle failures and relapses is a sign of strength rather than weakness. It is an essential part of your journey, training you to accept flaws and press on with persistence.

Handling Stressors from Without

Stressors from without are an unavoidable aspect of existence. They may originate from a variety of sources, including relationships, employment and health. It is essential that you manage these stressors if you want to keep your newly developed resilience and mental clarity.

We will look at useful methods in this part for managing stress from outside sources. You'll discover how to deal with life's obstacles by learning how to set limits, make reasonable expectations and use stress-reduction techniques. By becoming proficient in these techniques, you will build the resilience required to resist outside influences without giving in to anxiety and overanalyzing.

Recall that the goal is to improve your ability to manage pressures in your life without sacrificing your inner peace. It is not about getting rid of them.

Creating a Network of Support

Nobody should travel alone in search of inner tranquility. Creating a network of support is the last essential to your achievement. A support system, whether it comes from friends, family, or a group of people who share your values, is essential to overcoming setbacks and relapses.

I will assist you in developing a solid support network because I am an authority in this area. We'll talk about how to express your needs, ask for help when you need it and build a support system of people who get you on this path.

When things go tough, your network of support will serve as a safety net, offering you motivation, perspective and reassurance that you're not the only one pursuing resilience and mental clarity.

We will discuss the significance of managing setbacks and relapses, overcoming outside stressors and developing a support network in this last section. These are the abilities that will help you keep your newly discovered inner serenity while navigating the difficulties that are sure to arise. Come explore with me the transformational power of community, coping strategies and resilience. Together, we'll take the last steps toward living a life characterized by enduring mental clarity and emotional well-being.

CHAPTER 8

LIVING A LIFE OF FULFILLMENT AND FREEDOM

Setting and Achieving Personal Goals

The goal of mastering the technique of letting go of stress and overthinking is to live a life of fulfillment and freedom. It's a life characterized by accomplishment, meaning and deep satisfaction. Setting and accomplishing personal goals is the first step on the path to this destination.

Individual objectives are the benchmarks that drive us ahead and give us a sense of purpose. Our lives are shaped and our actions are motivated by our hopes, aspirations and wants. You will discover how to create attainable, purposeful goals that complement your beliefs and ambitions in this part.

I will assist you in creating a clear road map for your future by guiding you through the goal-setting process as a subject matter expert in this area. We'll look at techniques for dividing more ambitious goals into doable chunks and maintaining motivation as we go.

You will be freed from the constraints of overanalyzing and worrying if you can develop a purposeful and directed life and learn the art of creating and accomplishing personal goals.

Fostering an Understanding of Meaning and Purpose

A genuine sense of meaning and purpose is necessary for a life of fulfillment and freedom. It is the beacon of light that brightens your way and gives each day meaning. Finding and developing this feeling of purpose is a crucial step on your path to a more satisfying life.

You will discover how to discover your inner values, beliefs and passions in this section. You will go out on a voyage of self-discovery to uncover the special talents and contributions you may provide to the world. You will discover how to give your life meaning and purpose, from your relationships to your work, under the direction of a professional.

Living a life that is motivated by your innermost beliefs and goals requires developing a sense of meaning and purpose. You will be truly pleased with your life and find fulfillment in all that you do if you instill this sense of purpose into every day.

Adopting a Happy and Stress-Free Life

Finally, you will reach the highest point on your path: living a happy, worry-free life. This is your mission fulfilled, the result of all the work you put into learning how to let go.

You will possess the abilities to liberate yourself from the constraints of anxiety and overanalyzing by putting the concepts and techniques discussed in this book into practice. You will have developed the abilities to deal with life's obstacles gracefully and with resiliency. Additionally, you will have learned how to use mental clarity to solve problems, make decisions and joyfully savor every moment.

You can embrace a happy, worry-free life by making a commitment to personal development, evolution and self-awareness. It is a life that exudes positivity, meaning and freedom from the shackles of needless worry.

This last section will discuss the pleasures of living life to the fullest, which includes achieving personal objectives, having a deep sense of meaning and purpose and experiencing the sheer, unadulterated delight of living worry-free. Come celebrate with me the journey's transformative power and let's take the remaining steps toward a life filled with freedom and long-lasting fulfillment.

CONCLUSION

THE ONGOING JOURNEY TO INNER PEACE AND MENTAL CLARITY

I want to stress a key point as we come to the end of this life-changing adventure: finding inner calm and mental clarity is a continuous process. It is a continuous process, a lifetime dedication to personal development and self-discovery.

We have discussed the nuances of learning to let go of stress and overthinking throughout the pages of this book. We've studied these mental enemies in great detail, developed workable plans to defeat them and learned how to use mental clarity to live a happy and purposeful life.

However, it's important to keep in mind that finding inner peace is a way of life, not a destination. You have the chance to put the ideas and tactics you've learned here to use every day. Resilience, acceptance and mindfulness are continuous practices that can be improved upon and enhanced over time.

Motivation and Encouraging Words for the Path Ahead

I want to offer you my motivation and encouragement as you continue on your path to mental clarity and spiritual serenity. Recognize that you are capable of creating the life you want, free from the burden of pointless anxiety and overanalyzing. You underestimate your strength and you have boundless capacity for change.

When difficulties emerge and they unavoidably will, keep in mind the skills you have developed: the capacity for concentration, sound judgment, problem-solving and resilience. Accept the support system you've created for yourself and the people you've cultivated relationships with.

I can guarantee you that this adventure will yield incalculable benefits because I am an expert in this sector. You will lead a life filled with contentment, liberation and a deep feeling of joy if you can learn to let go. You'll leave behind a resilient and mentally clear legacy that will encourage others to find inner serenity.

Sources for Additional Research

As you continue on your path to mental clarity and inner calm, I've included a list of tools to help you along the way. These materials include books, workshops, courses and communities that can improve your comprehension and application of the concepts covered in this book.

I urge you to look out these materials and carry on learning about the practice of letting go. You will get more insight and experience greater personal progress the more you immerse yourself in this trip.

Finally, I would like to thank you for traveling with me on this life-changing adventure. It has been an honor to mentor you as you've learned to stop worrying and overanalyzing everything. As you move forward, never forget that you have limitless capacity for improvement and that seeking inner calm and mental clarity is a lifetime commitment.

May you have peace, clarity and a lasting feeling of fulfillment on your journey. You have the ability to influence not just your own life but also the lives of everyone you come in contact with, so seize every moment with passion and thankfulness. Cheers to a future characterized by the enduring happiness of living without worry.